Find
Yourself

Ways to Build Resilience

Through Self-Discovery

Dr. Frank Lawlis

This publication is offered for educational purposes only. It does not replace the advice of any medical or psychological professional. Should you need additional or personalized support, please reach out to a mental health professional.

Copyright © 2022 Frank Lawlis

All rights reserved.

ISBNs: 978-1-7326475-4-1 (paperback); 978-1-7326475-5-8 (ebook)

Edited by Jennifer Holder
https://fullbloompublications.com

Cover art is the original painting, Ecstasy © 2020 Lee Lawson
Lee@LeeLawson.com / https://www.LeeLawson.com

Cover and interior layout by Mayfly Design
https://mayflydesign.com

The life of a dreamer is full of hope and failures but never despair. I dedicate this book to my wife, Susan, as one who has kept my dreams alive.

Contents

Foreword **v**

Introduction: Pathways to Resilience **vii**

1 Honor Your Need to Retreat **1**

2 Draw Strength from Symbols of Who You Are **13**

3 Mark Changes with Rituals **23**

4 Let Music Move You Through Anything **33**

5 Find the Love in Loss **39**

6 Gather Resourcefulness from Inspirational Stories **51**

7 Continuously Spiral Toward Growth **59**

Conclusion: The Enduring Secret of Self-Discovery **67**

Further Reading **69**

Foreword

THE YEAR SPANNING FROM 2020 TO 2021 WAS ONE of the most challenging years of my life. I'm a woman, mother, mother-in-law, grandmother, entrepreneur, motivational coach, CEO of a company . . . and, like the rest of the world, I was hit with the global pandemic. I was confronted with one challenge after another, as in my family, we deal with mental illness. I am a mother of a son with mental illness. I felt so alone this last year, until I met Dr. Frank Lawlis.

For years I have watched him on the *Dr. Phil* show supervising and handling the world's most extreme cases of mental illness and brain care. I watched Dr. Lawlis endure some of the hardest human challenges globally. Like you perhaps, I also witnessed how people gained victorious recoveries with his stewardship. I thought, "Wow, I need to know this incredible man. Dr. Lawlis is a hero!"

This is not a regular book. *Find Yourself: Ways to Build Resilience Through Self-Discovery* is a human manual, in your back pocket, by your side, as your guiding light to redirect you in brain and body wellness. The step-by-step methods are designed to help you navigate life with a wealth of knowledge, experience, and instructional techniques that offer ancient and time-tested methods that have been scientifically proven over and over again.

Dr. Frank Lawlis has spent his life devoted to humankind and to the universe within each of us. The ritual routines in *Find Yourself* are filled with ways to listen to your soul in order to navigate challenges wisely. You will discover yourself through the practices, created to be like your own personal, human blueprint. They are handcrafted to help steer you through the challenges and dilemmas you face on a daily basis.

As presented in this masterful book, the message of resilience hits you right in the jugular, penetrating your mindset immediately. Aren't we seeking results and creative, vivid tools? In a pop-culture world, we want what we want, and we want it now. So "find yourself" and let the change begin. If you are seriously ready, so is your body, your mind, and your soul. As Dr. Lawlis says, "Our souls are vast enough to embrace all possibilities."

Christina Fulton
CEO, Immortal Beauty Inc.

Introduction

Pathways to Resilience

It amazes me how, when I look back on my life struggles, they turn out to have led to my life's greatest gifts. This is true of daily irritations, relationships gone awry, times when I felt directionless or unsure, and even when the world seemed to be falling apart. Each and every hardship has led me closer to my innermost self and my soul's desires for my life.

This self-knowledge has guided me to make really difficult decisions for my life. It tells me how to walk those first tentative steps toward learning to live without something or someone I have lost. While trying something new, even when I make a mistake, self-knowledge gives me what I need to try again a bit differently. I have now learned that this is all possible because struggling has put me in touch with my Inner Compass.

I like to think of our Inner Compass as the way our soul guides us and gives us direction. It allows us to work our way through hard times and not only emerge stronger for it but also grow happier. This Inner Compass is the most powerful tool I have, and boy has it been tested throughout my long life.

Time and time again, it turns out that I'm most miserable when I have lost touch with this Inner Compass. The grief of losses, rage at injustices, and confusion over events out of my control are horrible to endure—until I do one of the many practices in this book. Then I feel relief. My pain eases. Glimmers of motivation, even inspiration, shine light in total darkness. My life has not changed to make me feel better; circumstances are still rough going. What has changed is that I turned within, toward my inner wisdom, and found answers. Yes, a higher power guides us, but that voice speaks to our hearts . . . and our souls must be open to listening. So the answers to our hardships are found inside us, through self-discovery. With this book, I want to share these pathways to resilience with you.

This resilience is more than perseverance, as just trudging through an emotional swamp to get to the other side doesn't help you learn, grow, and strengthen. Perseverance is a way of waiting until your external circumstances change, until life changes. You endure. You carry on. You aren't in touch with meaning—in fact, little touches you because you are numb. When you are in pain and have lost touch with yourself, who you are, and your integrity, you lose so much physical and emotional energy that you become depressed and simply persevere. This happens because you are being untrue to yourself. If you don't turn inward to listen, you risk losing an important part of who you are, or even your whole self's purpose.

I invite you to begin a journey inward by becoming aware of where you are now. How do you fall on the resilience scale? The top of the scale can get you through anything, because you understand who you are, what is most meaningful to you, and you are in touch with the purpose of your life. On the lower end of the scale, you feel lost. This can be due to horrible things happening that traumatized you, or fear, confusion, or even self-neglect due to high demands from other people or your job. As you consider your response, see if the following statements about yourself are true right now.

1. My life has turned out worse than I hoped it would.
2. I feel out of control in my life.
3. I make bad choices for my life; my judgment is terrible.
4. I feel I am living a lie.
5. I feel I am just marking time as it goes by.
6. My life has no special meaning.
7. I am experiencing mental or spiritual pain.
8. The challenges in my life depress me.
9. I don't know where my life is heading and that scares me.
10. My goals seem to fall away amidst challenges.
11. When I begin a new day, I just want to retreat from it.
12. I feel trapped in a lifestyle that is not true to who I am.
13. I cannot describe myself with words that positively describe who I am. (Can you?)
14. I cannot recall three events that gave me great joy. (Can you?)

All of these statements have been made by people on the low end of the resiliency scale. If more than half of these sound like something you might say, know that the people who spoke these things eventually rediscovered themselves, gained fresh options for their lives, and were able to resolve their pain in ways that led to happiness. Simply persevering through your struggles hoping for a return to "normalcy" is not a vibrant, enriching, inspiring, change-inducing, nor wish-fulfilling way to live. So what is?

With this book, I want to share the tools for resiliency, not perseverance. Not only does resiliency help you bounce back into shape, when you use hardship to get in touch with your self and your Inner Compass, resiliency also means you come back smarter, stronger, and more inspired than ever before. Knowing the secret to resiliency has helped me live in a way that I take pride in. I look back and see that a greater wisdom was always with me, even in my darkest hours. Confidence in that has meant everything to me. I feel self-discovery and our Inner Compass are the most powerful resources we have, and so I want you to gain access also.

This book is filled with ways to listen to your soul in order to navigate challenges wisely. I base practices I offer my patients, and you, on ancient and time-tested methods that scientific research and my clinical experience also support. I find they appeal to the deepest evolutionary parts of ourselves and also offer great opportunities to face our modern challenges and dilemmas in timeless ways. They open us up to the possibility of infinity within us, which is a fancy way of saying that our souls are vast enough to embrace all possibilities.

So join me on this journey. Do the practices in this book. And find your own inner resources that will keep you thriving, no matter what.

Honor Your Need to Retreat

BEING ALIVE TODAY MOST OFTEN MEANS BEING busy, and I think that's a regrettable fact. Things move so fast that we must juggle many aspects of our lives, of who we are and what's important to us, in speedy and efficient ways. While efficiency makes for a productive society as we race to complete tasks with as little energy or effort possible, I feel it leaves people unhappy. We have no time to linger on what we do, appreciating it and even seeking deeper meaning in it. This leads to so many challenges, including feeling burned out in work, relationships with family and friends, and even in spiritual matters. We don't even have time to process our feelings—and when so much is happening, our natural emotional responses get so overwhelming that we stuff them, ignore them, or distract ourselves from them.

With all this going on, it's no wonder things clash. Maybe one area of your life is taking over the rest. Perhaps things that are important to you are being neglected. Or could a general sense of being too stressed to cope be making your anger fuse short? Even if your life has exploded with a catastrophe you can't control, your pain about it may halt any steps to minimize damage. Simply put, the intensity of life can be too much to bear.

I see headlines in popular magazines that offer advice for this. They encourage you to become even more efficient by organizing your possessions, multitasking through technology, managing time with an app, or even seeking balance by adding more daily self-care tasks to your list. But there is a simple technique that is as old as time, humanity, and organized religion. We all need to retreat.

Honestly, you may crave retreat so much that all I need to do is give you permission to do it. Perhaps you know exactly what you need: a day in bed, time alone to paint, going for a solo walk in a beautiful place, or booking a remote cabin where you can do whatever you feel like doing. If you can hear that inner voice screaming at you to "Pause!" "Stop!" "Slow down!" then you must honor it.

Once you have stepped back, into retreat, away from the world and everything that can distract you from yourself, the transformative magic can happen. I have done this enough in my own life and have seen it in thousands of patients' lives: whatever you do, or whatever happens to you or within you, you will come out of retreat transformed in some way. While I call this magic, what's really happening is that you remove barriers to listening to yourself. A higher power can speak, and your soul can listen. Your soul can communicate your needs and what's important. Then you can dream about changes you might like to make. Things you want to do differently, or more of. Inspirations seem to fall from the sky, and while they might seem nonsensical or weird, they have messages for you.

The result of retreat is deepened insights into what is going on in your life and the world, and how you can navigate better in all ways. Any challenge you face—yes, anything—can be met with the spirit of resilience that you inherently have. You realize that your hardship is workable, that you actually have what it takes to tackle a problem, and that you can, and will, use the challenge as an opportunity for change. Therefore, because you retreated into solitude and reflection, you won't just cope or persevere. Your life will become better, and you will grow stronger in who you are.

Consider Jesus walking for forty days, battling temptation, sitting in long hours of meditation as part of His mission of love. The Buddha sitting alone, with eyes closed, gaining enlightenment. Or Einstein's solitary daydreaming that developed his revolutionary treatise on physics. Practices in our religions, arts, and sciences, as well as stories within many biographies, show that with long periods of isolation, we emerge with insights that change our whole worldview in spectacular ways.

As you begin the path of self-discovery that leads to resiliency, I want to not only encourage retreat, I also want to help you direct it for maximum benefit. You have the capacity to discover truth, whether about your self, the world, or spiritual realms, through private interactions with your inner depths.

I want to share two different ways to engage yourself in retreat. These methods work powerfully for me and will get you started on the right foot with yourself. They both involve solitude and isolation. The first makes the most of nature's power to heal as you engage its elements. The second silences all stimuli outside your body so you can sense, be, and listen.

Over time you will be able to design your own retreats, giving yourself exactly what you need because you can hear inner messages from your higher power, soul, and Inner Compass. They don't speak more loudly in solitude; rather you have learned to slow down, pay attention, and listen. If you retreat enough, eventually you will receive messages in your day-to-day life. Once you can do that, I have found, you will feel truly alive and be most resilient. All because you have gained a skill for staying true to who you are.

Call on the Elements to Support Your Retreat

Our souls crave the perspective on our problems that comes with connecting to something larger than our personal self. And there is no healing power greater than the Earth. So I invite you to turn to her and draw on her resourcefulness. She has the ability to provide the exact remedy you need, whether you seek it physically, mentally, or spiritually.

In this section, I will guide you to connect with the Earth's elements on all three of these levels. The elements of fire, water, air, and earth each have different effects and can be drawn on for different purposes. For example:

- If you are heartbroken over a breakup or divorce and need the warmth of love, call on fire.
- If you are surrounded by negativity at work and need to cleanse yourself of it, connect with water.
- If you experienced a great loss, such as the death of someone close to you, invoking the spaciousness of air can help lighten your spirit.
- And if you have been carrying a great load, whether through trauma, overworking, or anything that causes you extreme stress, you can call on earth to support you.

The elements are basic, direct, and simple—their qualities reach us on an instinctual level that goes right through our thoughts and feelings about what's happening in our lives. We simply need to open our senses and feel gratitude for nature.

I invite you to try the methods I suggest first. Then once you have a sense of how each element affects you, create your own way of relating with them as best meets your needs. This is your journey of resilience, so be creative and act on the guidance you receive.

The Element of Fire

Fire powerfully evokes passion, love, and creativity. By simply gazing at a warming blaze in a darkened space, like a candle or bonfire, you can experience peace and tranquility in the midst of anything that you are going through. I recommend starting with fire because its warmth can soothe and reassure you as you begin to open up, soften, and listen to your soul. Here are some ways to call on the healing power of fire.

Pay attention to your body: While you don't want to harm your eyes by staring directly into a flame, you can soften your gaze so that you are observing everything in front of you. Also focus to the side of the flame or above it, and you will still witness the flame dancing with currents of air. Allow feelings like joy or playfulness to arise in response, just noticing changes in how you feel for now.

Then feel the flame's warmth on your skin. Hold your hands up to it, or if you have a fire going in a fireplace or firepit, just allow the radiance to enfold you. Notice how your body responds: Do your muscles relax? Do you feel soothed? Maybe stress seems to melt from your limbs and torso. Perhaps a sense of overall well-being arises, which may make you realize how much your body has been affected by the stress of your hardship.

Let sensations wash over you . . . just notice them.

Pay attention to your emotions: The flicker of the flames will also warm your emotions. You may have chosen a coping strategy in an attempt to protect yourself and persevere. These can include becoming frozen, stuck, numb, or feeling urges to withdraw and avoid. As you sit with fire, these forms of armor will soften . . . just allow it to happen. Let yourself recall what it felt like to live fully, joyfully, and with the full engagement of vibrant emotions. We feel alive when emotions are allowed to arise and express, so let anything stopping them melt away.

Once this armor melts, as you feel warm and safe in your solitude, let the emotions come. Feel them. Let them express. What has been going on within you that you have been ignoring or keeping yourself protected from? Let fire tend to you as you cry, scream, rage, shout, plead, pray. Stand up and stomp your feet, reach for the heavens, shake your limbs, or punch the air. Dancing flames will support your movement, so allow emotions to move through you and release by moving your body. This is cathartic, helpful, and healing.

Let emotions wash through you . . . just allow them to move.

Pay attention to your thoughts: All this time, as you feel sensations and emotions, thoughts will arise. Your worries, doubts, ruminations, or fears are likely to come to the surface of your mind. The difference between thinking these things in an ordinary way and thinking them now is that you have the help of fire. These thoughts might sting or cause you to flinch, so offer them to the fire. You can make an offering gesture with your hand, imagining that the painful thought is in your grip. Simply open your hand and drop it into the flame.

As you do, your mind will naturally become as warmed and relaxed as your body. Overthinking and any intellectual explanations for the challenges you are facing will fall away. This makes space for deeper thoughts to arise. Perhaps you will notice deeply held beliefs about why you can't face the hardship or that hold you back from learning and growing. Let your mind become a gentle witness, with the gentle, kind, compassionate quality of a calm flame. This will invite the clarity and focus of fire—as light in the dark—that offers the peace you need to gain clarity and insight.

The Element of Water

You shower or bathe as part of your ritual for taking care of your body and leaving the house to go to work, school, or to be social. Cleansing dirt and sweat from your skin with water is just part of daily life. But I encourage you to explore a deeper relationship with water, both within your routine and also more intentionally evoking its healing power.

Water is cleansing and purifying for your entire being: body, mind, and spirit. Since ancient times, and around the world, people have bathed before rituals or prayer. You too can increase potency by arriving at sacred moments in your life by first engaging with water. It can be a whole-body scrub or a more symbolic gesture of rinsing your hands. This helps you let go of impurities, including negative attitudes like doubt, anxiety, aggression, or even selfishness or misplaced ambition. All you need to do is set this intention by thinking something like, "May I be cleansed of all negativity" or "May anything that may obscure wise insight wash away." Then engage with water, and as it flows across your skin, imagine pain leaving you with it.

I feel water is so powerful because it flows over and around everything, teaching us along the way. This is why watching it move can be powerfully healing. Water can make incredibly beautiful scenery, so as part of your solitude go sit beside a lake, a river, in a canyon, or on a beach. Witness water in its natural form as it moves and interacts with the environment. Rivers can teach you about flowing across obstacles unimpeded. Oceans inspire feelings of vastness and perspective as waves rise, crest, and fall as far as the eye can see. Lakes are sources of inspiration as light dances across them, everything is reflected in them, and animals gather to drink from them. The possibilities for what water can teach you are endless. And just sitting quietly beside it, in solitude, can inspire serenity and inner quiet. Sometimes that is all we need.

The Element of Air

Breathe in. Then release the air through your mouth with a long, slow exhale. You will instantly feel lighter and more alert. The air element evokes intelligence. It also brings feelings of harmony, as breathing unites us all. And our primary means of communication, speaking, relies on air currents passing over our vocal cords. So to benefit from the healing power of air, sometimes all you need to do is take a deep breath . . . or three.

I see terrific results when I engage the scents that ride on air to stimulate people with smells. As the most sensitive of human senses, smell reaches our innermost selves—and can therefore transform us in body, mind, and spirit. Aromas appeal to the most urgent and sensitive brain region, so they can stimulate us neurologically. Instantly. Try it; you'll see. All you need is your spice cabinet or perhaps some essential oils. Try lavender, peppermint, cinnamon, pine, vanilla, and pumpkin aromas. Then notice how you feel. If you find a favorite, just take a tissue, put a few drops of the scent on it, and seal it in a plastic bag. Then you can carry it with you for a whole-being refresh in any moment.

Within your retreat setting, choose an aroma that causes

you to feel a pleasant emotion. Then recall an image or a scene that is troubling you, perhaps causing you anxiety or depression. Holding that image in mind, deeply inhale your aroma through your nose. Take at least two sniffs. You will likely feel instant relief from the pain caused by the memory. Notice how it feels to let go of your troubles and surrender them to the positive experience of your favored aroma.

Doing this in solitude creates powerful connections in your nervous system. From then on, as you go about your life and negative emotion overwhelms you, you can take out your aroma and disrupt the negativity. Surrender to letting go. And embrace positive experience. In other words, you will have a powerful tool for halting what could become a downward emotional spiral. Instead, you can go about your day in a more positive state. This is an instantaneous method for invoking the healing air element as it interacts intimately with your nervous system.

The Element of Earth

Sometimes when we're suffering and surrounded by hardship, it can feel like the ground fell out from beneath our feet. We don't know what to do, where to turn, or even if anything can help us. We feel confused and unstable. This is when the earth element can help.

Feeling unstable in life can sometimes feel like a personal emergency. What you may need is to shift your attention to the ground beneath you. It is supporting you, it is holding you, and you just need to connect with that basic fact of gravity. This can be done instantly, wherever you are. If you are standing, feel your feet on the ground. If you are walking, connect with the sensations on the bottom of your feet as you take each step. If you are sitting, feel where your seat connects with your body's weight. The ground is always there—and you can count on it. Feeling this in your body will stabilize you, and a confidence in your ability to face the moment will increase. It's as if the earth says, "I got you. I'll hold you steady through this." Hearing that message can be a huge relief.

I recommend keeping a garden of some kind as part of the time you spend in solitude. The earth element is also associated with fertility and nourishment. While yes, you can grow nutritious food, even if you keep a planter with some flowers, you can benefit from engaging the earth. All kinds of health problems, including stress, depression, and anxiety, have been shown to ease after we dig in the earth. The reasons are manifold: the minerals in the soil, the grounded feeling of digging in earth, the peace of being outside relating with nature, and the creativity of tending plants. So as you plan time for yourself, consider gardening.

Go Deep Within Through Sensory Deprivation

Solitude is incredibly powerful, for better or for worse. When left entirely alone, we can resolve deep inner issues, or we can torture ourselves in a downward spiral of thinking. This is why I recommend that you begin your retreat practice, and your relationship with your self, by engaging with the elements. Once you establish a relationship with nature's healing forces, you can feel safe enough within yourself to venture deeper.

Sensory deprivation is the best method I know to allow your soul's wisdom to surface. This wisdom is the initial point of contact with your Inner Compass. I highly recommend this process because it can lead to insights that inspire complete freedom and choice in your life. This is especially important when you are in the midst of difficult times, because circumstances can block your inner knowing. Then you feel lost. And when you are lost, you make choices that can harm yourself or others. So in your effort to find yourself, it helps to reduce all forms of distraction—including from your own body—and go deep enough within that you can access your wisdom resources.

I have seen all kinds of things happen when people enter the still quiet of sensory deprivation. As you enter your depths, you may:

- Emerge with insights into a traumatic past that help you build a fresh future
- Find deep sources of motivation to make changes that will turn your life around
- Hold imaginary conversations with people who have hurt you, to reach forgiveness
- Connect with mythical or symbolic sources of power, such as a spirit animal, gods or goddesses, nature spirits, or angels
- Hear direction from God about your soul's purpose or the meaning of your life
- Recall dreams for your life that you had as a child, but then forgot
- Feel long stuffed or ignored emotions release in transformative ways

Creating a sensory deprivation experience can be simple or elaborate. Sometimes wisdom is hovering just below the surface of consciousness, waiting for an hour of our attention to arise. You can try sitting in a quiet room with your eyes closed. You might need to tie a scarf across your eyes and wear earplugs. Or you can take a camping mattress or pillows into a closet and lie down. You can also schedule time in a sensory deprivation float tank, if there is one in your town. The popularity of these increases and decreases, but they can have tremendous effects. Just remember the purpose: no sight, no scent, no sound, no taste, and as little touch as is possible so you can reach the center of your being.

As you prepare to enter this meditative state, it helps to set an intention. At the least, intend to connect with your inner wisdom or higher power. You can enter with the resolve to gain insight into the specific challenge you are facing. And you can always set the stage for healing by first calling on the aid of one or more of the elements: perhaps fire for self-compassion, water for cleansing negativity, air for a fresh perspective, and earth for strength.

Then, when you enter your sensory deprivation experience, drop all expectations for what might happen within you. Be open to what arises. Stay curious about where you are led to explore. And above all, remain kind to yourself as you allow the journey to unfold.

Draw Strength from Symbols of Who You Are

"Who am I?" can be a daunting question when you try to answer it with your thinking mind. I've found that people tend to think about who they are in interesting ways, and you probably do too. Most of us avoid asking this question at all, preferring to exist reactively, habitually, mechanically. In terms of your experience, you could say your self is what bounces from event to event as you do the best you can to cope. But that view fosters perseverance only, without the wise insights of your Inner Compass as you navigate hardship. If you want true resilience, I encourage you to view your self as an endless resource.

If that sounds strange, just consider all the times in life when you were so challenged you thought you'd never get through it. And then you did. Somehow, you put one foot in front of the other and continued. You were drawing on deep resources within you that you didn't know you had. Now, imagine knowing those resources were there, so you could turn inward to draw on them at any time.

The abundance of our inner resourcefulness is infinite, but this feels hard to grasp unless we apply our imaginations to give each resource a relatable form, shape, concept, and even personality. Then you can use your senses to visualize, evoke, pray to, or call the name of exactly the help you need. This chapter gives you some practices you can do to relate with who you are through the power of symbols.

A Symbol for Your Life

Take note of the fact that symbols surround us. They have all kinds of meanings around the world. All nations have an emblem and specific colors on their flags. In the US, political parties have donkey and elephant symbols. Sports teams have their mascots. There are spiritual symbols, such as the Christian cross, the Jewish six-pointed Star of David, and the five-pointed Druid Pentacle. Locales and families have had them, whether through clan plaid tartans or elaborate crests. Gigantic book volumes have been published with the single purpose of identifying the seemingly infinite symbols from throughout human history.

Symbols have a language of their own, in that they communicate meaning on preverbal, instinctual levels. Science is showing that we are affected neurologically by certain symbols, like the circle and a lattice. Our bodies respond to them in a way that suggests we are born receptive to them. And those responses grow through exposure throughout our lives—just think of how you may tear up at the sight of an American flag, especially if you are a veteran. Symbols are impressed deeply upon us, so I suggest harnessing this power to understand who we are.

When you identify a personal symbol, or a series of symbols for different parts of your being, you can intentionally draw on it. It becomes a portal to your innermost being, to your soul, for whatever you need, whenever you need it. These personal symbols can be elaborate or as simple as a circle, spiral, square, triangle, and cross.

Instead of actively creating a personal symbol, I encourage you to allow symbols to emerge from within your mind's eye. They are most potent when it feels like they find you, magically and intuitively, rather than analyzing the meaning or selecting one from a book. All you need is a blank piece of paper and pen and a quiet space where you can be alone. Here are the steps.

1. Enter a state of retreat, deep relaxation, and inner listening, as I guided you to do in chapter 1.
2. Allow your mind to relax and expand, holding the intention for a personal symbol to arise. Let thoughts come and go, even allow a few symbols to arise and fall away as you get past the layers of your rational mind.
3. When the symbol you are looking for comes into your mind, you will know it. You will feel its power and immediately perceive the meaning it conveys with your whole-being awareness.
4. Don't seek to analyze or intellectualize it yet—instead, open your eyes and draw it on the blank piece of paper. Be with it, alert to the sensations in your body.
5. Only later, when you have emerged from the retreat space, do you want to look it up or think about what it means.

When I did this, what emerged was a set of concentric circles divided into four sections with a star in the center. Years later, I still feel its power as it has only grown more potent with time and use. That is the most important part, but I did research the history of this symbol with fascinating results. It was apparently an ancient symbol of God, was used to indicate the union of man and woman in sacred bonds, and has been a symbol of the North Star that once helped humans navigate the seas. For me, the symbol offers me guidance as I navigate the four seasons of life.

Once you have received your personal symbol, you can draw on it for resilience. The mere act of visualizing it can center you when you feel off-balance, infuse you with energy when you feel drained, recall your deepest motivations for completing a task when you want to give up, and remind you of what values you stand for when faced with a decision that challenges your sense of what's right, wrong, or appropriate for a given situation. It will become a living part of your psyche, so allow it to show up as it will—and then receive what its power conveys to you.

A System of Self-Awareness

Each and every one of us has both strengths and weaknesses in our personality. No exceptions. You probably have many personality traits you are proud of and some you may regret or hide—even from yourself. You may be unaware of aspects of your style that other people see clearly. Personality traits are extremely varied and unique, but the fact remains that you cannot have all the good ones.

Insights into your style help you understand the things you do and the things you avoid. They help you recognize patterns in your thinking, feeling, and acting that lead to making different future choices, learning from mistakes, growing from experience, knowing when to ask for help from others, and setting a situation up for your success. All this supports self-awareness, which is an essential part of resilience. Knowing your personality's strengths and weaknesses helps you think creatively and resourcefully to navigate any challenge or hardship.

Personality traits are related to each other and, as a whole, create personality types. Psychologists use several personality questionnaires, and it might serve you well to see a professional to learn more about yourself. But you can also conduct your own self-analysis using a system with ancient roots called the Enneagram. It divides all personality traits into nine general types. Here is a short summary of each, and you can choose which one of the nine you feel you are *at this time*. Then, as you change through the years, you can reassess.

Type 1: The Perfectionist. Searching for perfection, avoiding error; uses words such as "should," "must," and "ought to"; compulsively works to block internal guilt; superb powers of discernment; severe critic to self and others.

Type 2: The Giver. Needs approval from others; avoids own needs; pride in being needed; confusion in knowing the "real me"; wants freedom; self-preservation falters to meet the needs of others.

Type 3: The Performer. Motivated by achievement; a producer; loves achieving goals; competitive and efficient; feels "I am what I do"; maximizes success.

Type 4: The Romantic. Attracted to moods; disdains *ordinary* life for the different, high-fantasy life; dramatic; feelings of abandonment and loss; emotional sensitivity; prone to depression and drama.

Type 5: The Observer. Preoccupied with privacy; guards over one's time; knowledge; makes do with less to gain independence; keeps life in departments; analytical; has the power of *knowing*.

Type 6: The Devil's Advocate. Procrastinating; avoids action, high goals; anxiety peaks with success; authority problems; skeptic, doubt about everything; says "Yes, but..."; scans the world for clues of inner fear; looks for the worst outcome.

Type 7: The Option-Seeker. Wants stimulation and excitement; fun seeking, maintains multiple options; charm as a major interpersonal attraction; dislikes commitment; creative; wants to experience everything in life.

Type 8: The Boss. Always in need of control; seeks possessions and power; concerned with justice; avoids weakness; mistrust of others; aggressive, denies other points of view; "all or nothing" attitude.

Type 9: The Mediator. Comforts self with small pleasures; ambivalence about personal decisions in seeking group consensus; postpones change with repeating solutions; can't say "no"; controls by being stubborn; sees all sides to problems; passive-aggressive.

As you consider these personality styles, you may see how you express different traits in different situations. And on a deep level, all of them will be familiar, as we are all ultimately all of these types. After you decide which type you express most, ask three or four friends to consider it too. There will likely be differences in what they see, as their perceptions may reveal things you are unconscious of. The things you agree about represent your conscious self. From this self-knowledge, you can strengthen your resiliency to deal with life's challenges.

Your Spirit Animal

Each animal's characteristics are unique, and it has compelling abilities specific to its species. For example, an eagle can soar in the highest wind currents—and therefore sees a vast vision of life. A coyote can trick prey and hunters—demonstrating how a clever twist on things can be the answer to a challenge. And a mother bear's protectiveness of her cubs shows us to cherish and guard things we love. We can observe how animals behave in nature and learn from them.

You can draw on this to form a special, symbolic relationship with an animal species. In moments of vulnerability, whenever you feel weakened, or if you don't know what to do, you can ask a spirit animal for help. Around the world and throughout time, people have seen animals as spiritual guides. We share the earth with them, and their particular wisdom about living can support our own ability to navigate life. Here is a simple method to connect with a spirit animal. It helps to listen to a drumbeat, at four beats per second, and to do this exercise for just ten minutes.

1. In your retreat space, relax deeply until your mind is quiet. As peace surrounds you, open your imagination and see yourself walking the earth in search of a hole in it. It can be a rabbit hole, snake hole, cave, even a pool of water or lake.
2. Dive down the hole, remembering that this is your spiritual self, so size makes no difference. Continue through the earthly passage, using the drumbeat as guidance, until you pop out into a lower realm of the earth.
3. Imagine sitting in a space, perhaps surrounded by trees, looking out on the ocean, or beside a stream—whatever environment you perceive. Be patient and wait until any animals start approaching. Some may wander off, but one of these may be your spirit animal.
4. If an animal stays with you or returns three times, ask if it is your guide. If so, you may ask some questions, but be brief. You can return again.
5. When the drum changes its cadence, or almost ten minutes have passed, it is time to return. Go back the way you arrived, returning through the tunnel, and open your eyes.
6. Write down your experience in detail. Everything has symbolic meaning. Then draw or write about your animal spirit guide. What did he or she look like? How did he walk? What did she say? Did they do anything? Take you anywhere? These are all messages for your life, so begin to listen.

7. Give thanks to your spirit animal by dancing, singing, reciting a poem, or writing a letter. Honor the experience in some way, because your gratitude will increase a spirit animal's power within you.

I have experienced so much insight, healing, and wisdom thanks to my spirit animal. From your retreat space, you can close your eyes and descend into the lower realm of the earth to visit your spirit animal at any time. You need to try it to experience the power and wisdom that comes through. Once you do, you'll never have to face life challenges alone, as there is always a source of counsel. That promise alone offers a potent source of resilience.

Mark Changes with Rituals

OUR LIVES ARE FILLED WITH RITUALS. CHANGE IS something humanity has always marked with holidays, celebrations, grieving periods, and ceremonies. I think that in the grand scheme of history and our lives, we do this because change is something that feels hard.

Even positive change comes with some degree of hardship. You may land your dream job, but it's in a faraway city, and you need to move away from things and people you love. You might meet the person you want to marry, but the two of you need to figure out how to merge finances, households, even families, and navigate each other's personal living habits. We celebrate people on their birthdays, with parties, gifts, and cake, but it also means they are aging—which comes with all kinds of challenging feelings. This is why we need to pay more attention to the rituals that mark our lives, create new ones, and bring back those lost to time.

Honoring change with rituals is a powerful resilience practice. It not only helps you get through the hardship along the way, it also motivates you to stay true to your Inner Compass as you make decisions at each step. It helps transition your sense of who you are, as you make life changes, so you are not stuck in old patterns of thought, emotion, and behavior that might become stumbling blocks. This chapter shares rituals you can use to strengthen your resilience by acknowledging that there are true challenges around every corner in life and that you have what you need to meet those challenges with wisdom and purpose.

Honor Annual Cultural Rituals

We mark the passage of time on birthdays, anniversaries, and New Year's Eve. Throughout the year, we honor national leaders with holidays and send forms of appreciation to our mothers and fathers. Religious observances have many forms and evoke virtuous themes such as new hope and love at Christmas, the triumph of lightness over darkness at Diwali, atonement and purification at Yom Kippur, and praying to be closer to God at Ramadan. These dates remind us of cultural history and the values we hold dear.

As annual events on our calendars, they happen almost automatically. I feel their regularity causes us to take them lightly, not as personally, so we don't feel their themes as deeply as we otherwise might. But if you look at these events as rituals, instead of just another day passing by, you can add meaning to your life.

Religious holidays, and even planetary events like solstices and equinoxes, can teach us about what each season in nature has to offer: spring is when we experience renewal and fresh starts, summer is when we get to play and rejoice, autumn is when we appreciate what we have and let go of what we no longer need, and winter is when we rest, clarify what we want, and dream of what might happen in the next cycle.

These are profound because they are also the seasons within our psyches. Just as each year plants are born, grow, mature, and die, so do we.

There can be great wisdom in the way we do things, but sometimes it requires that we look past the mundane and seek out the sacred. Any ritual you do can be a burden, chore, or obligation. That same ritual, say celebrating your daughter's sixth birthday, if done with sacred vision, can be a powerful experience of appreciation and celebration.

This simple mindset flip can make each year pass more joyously and meaningfully. If things are challenging or going wrong, the holiday can be an invitation to pause, retreat, reflect, and reconnect with your soul and your higher power. You will refill your energy capacity and can continue on with resilience.

Navigate Any Change Intentionally

Life is full of transitions. In fact, sometimes I think life is one constant transition from one state of being into the next. But if you break it down, in terms of life events, after being born you learn to walk. Then you go to school. You pass through puberty, get your driver's license, and graduate from high school. After that, you may earn degrees, get your first job on a career ladder, get married, and then your first baby may be born. You mark your children's milestones and celebrate their successes. Your career has ups and downs, your home life has challenges and joys, but all the while every year, you mark the fact that you are aging.

Every single one of these transitions can call for a ritual, whether a rite of passage or a celebration. Within healthy transitions that lead to significant life changes, I see three phases. If you can navigate change by honoring each phase as part of a change ritual, your hardship will ease, and you will be prepared to embrace new directions with a refreshed sense of who you are. This is a resilience that can help you learn, grow, and age happily.

Phase 1: Prepare for Change

Don't overlook the importance of gearing up to achieve something you care about. For a wedding, you choose a venue, invite guests, and rehearse the ceremony. You study national history and law when seeking to become a citizen of a new country. Applying to college kicks off dreams for what adult life could be like. Taking these preparations to heart holds you accountable to yourself as you realize what behavior changes will be required of you. You are learning, gathering, and experiencing—all so you will be ready for change once it's here.

This is when it is important to research your options, listen to your soul, and check in with your Inner Compass because this phase is when you set your course. Make sure it aligns with your deepest knowing by going into retreat (chapter 1) and checking in with your sense of who you are (chapter 2). Then, when this exploratory and learning phase concludes, you will have a clear decision about the direction your life is taking. Knowing you chose it—wholeheartedly—empowers you, strengthens you, and increases your sense of agency in life.

Phase 2: Transition Through Change

Even if there is a ceremony involved, which you begin in one state of being (single, citizen of one country, high school graduate) and emerge in another state (married, citizen of a different country, college freshman), there is a dramatic transition phase. This is when your self takes on a whole new social personality. Within almost any context, there are new roles to fill, expectations to satisfy, rules to abide by, and standards someone expects you to uphold. No amount of preparation eliminates a sense of shock at this new way of being. New family members, bosses, friends, even stores if you moved—all ask you to be different from how you were.

It may come as a surprise, but you must allow yourself to grieve for who you were, what you left behind to pursue something else, and maybe even for the new self you must become. Strong emotions can arise during this phase: anger, sadness, guilt, shame. You might find yourself exhausted, sleeping more. Or you might be elated and feel high on life. Just know that however you process the transition is okay; your emotions might seem misplaced, but you are engaging a tremendously potent period of change in your life. Have compassion for all the parts of you that need to come to terms with what has happened, that need to catch up. Deep down, we're complex. So be sure to retreat and check in with your self often.

Phase 3: Celebrate Outcomes and Learn Lessons

Sometimes this third phase of transformation in a change ritual can be overwhelmed by the drama of the transition phase. Don't let that happen. After the sudden shift in interpersonal relationships, with new people and new expectations, a higher level of self-regard develops.

You will find you have new priorities in life. These can be major challenges to how you previously defined yourself and how others perceived you before. This is when celebrating a change is essential for resiliency going forward. If you stayed true to your sense of self and who you are all along the way, marking it with celebration can be an empowering way to start sharing this new life with others. Some people enjoy celebrating with parties, by popping the champagne, cooking up a delicious meal, or having meaningful discussions with close loved ones. Some prefer to reflect quietly, allowing the feeling of accomplishment to be their celebration.

Once you've basked, be sure to consider what you learned along the way. The real shift within you comes when it's time to write a new script for your life based on the change you have made. You will surely need these lessons in your new life, so write them down and keep them close. This way, you will continue to grow—and never stagnate or be stuck—as you navigate change with resiliency.

Recapture from Trauma or Mental Paralysis

While I said earlier that all change feels hard, there are experiences in life that cause excruciating wounds. If you were deeply hurt in any way, you may not feel equipped to deal with life because you are too afraid. This can even lead to what I refer to as mental paralysis: when facing situations that call for change and growth, you might retreat to a safer condition instead and become trapped there.

Mental paralysis is a state of survival, where you can hide to avoid new experiences. You feel the need to do this because of shame, for what happened, who you are, and what you deep-down want from life. Or you may stay in this state because it is safe (employment rather than starting your own business), it may have once given you pride (like being varsity quarterback as a teenager), your family taught you it was the right way to live (like being a stay-at-home mom), or because you won't be judged if you just pretend to be different from who you truly are.

Pain can cause all of us to develop habits that we think protect us, but that actually only hurt us more and lock us in a wounded state. If you have been deeply hurt, until you heal, you will persevere just to endure the ongoing hard knocks to your spirit. This is utterly exhausting. This can all change with ritual.

This ritual helps resolve trauma. It comes from ancient healing methods that recover lost parts of yourself. Traumatic experience causes something within us to run and hide—so far within our psyches that we forget they're there. But within your imagination, you can go in search of these lost parts. Just finding them is powerful, but you can also welcome them, speak with them, and listen to their messages for you. This way, fragmented pieces of you can return to a sense of wholeness. And become resources within you to help you live more resiliently.

Traumatic experiences, especially in childhood, can affect your sense of who you are, what you can do in life, and even whether you deserve it when good things happen. Trauma in childhood tends to make you feel unsafe as an adult. You may have been born in a family that passes down forms of physical or psychological abuse from generation to generation, reenacting history's pain within each new child. Your family may have passed on limiting beliefs or highly critical voices that continue on in your mind long after you have left home. All this can lead you to be traumatized into self-doubt and low self-esteem, which can rule your life—leaving you trapped by a traumatic past. Any attempt to venture forth, into new possibilities, can be too scary and painful, so once again you retreat. You hide. And you become lost to yourself.

This is why I recommend that you first do this self-recapturing ritual with the intention to find your lost child self. Your younger, child self is hiding somewhere in your psyche, unable to express the playful creativity and curiosity that drives children's activities. By finding this child, you can bring these qualities back into your life, which will make change so much easier to navigate. Rather than hide from new things, you can become excited by exploration and possibility. Just like the ritual I shared earlier for navigating changes in life, this ritual has three phases.

Phase 1: Preparation to Meet a Lost Part of Your Self

Plan to enter the retreat space you created for yourself in chapter 1. Like the journey for a spirit animal in chapter 2, this whole ritual takes place within your imagination. Within this psychological, imaginative space, similar to dreams, there are no rules like gravity or social rules holding you back. Nature and objects can speak, for example. So that you do not see this lack of conventional logic and structure as frightening, prepare by *setting your intention* and then *finding someone to guide you*.

Your intention is a simple statement that anchors your experience in imaginative space. It is the answer to questions like: What lost part of yourself do you want to find? What question do you want the answer to? What help do you need to overcome an obstacle? If this were a treasure hunt, your intention would be the treasure you are seeking, the purpose of the journey. In psychological space, treasure comes in the form of information about who you are and how to overcome obstacles—therefore increasing your resilience. But there is no map for the location of this information; it is a mystery. Because of this, you must be willing to open your mind to discovery and awe. With trauma, forging into any unknown space can feel dangerous—even within your mind.

So find a guide. This guide can be a real-life friend who listens to you narrate what you experience, coaches you along, and reminds you of your intention. While they are blind to your experiences, speaking what you see aloud can feel grounding and safe, and their empathy can be soothing. Or you can imagine a guide, like your spirit animal from chapter 2, or perhaps a spiritual guide like Jesus or Buddha, or even someone from your past who was a mentor like a sports coach or classroom teacher. With your eyes closed, visualize this guide in front of you, share your intention with them, and ask for their help.

Phase 2: Engaging the Imaginative Journey

Relax your fears, as your mind can be aware of the room you are sitting in and also an imaginative world at the same time, while not absorbed into either. Close your eyes. Your guide can lead you to a doorway. In your imagination, the doorway may lead to a building, the sky, the earth, into a tree or a mountainside. Follow your guide and pass through the threshold, stepping into whatever your psychological space looks like. Perhaps it's a landscape, a place you recognize from your past, or somewhere fantastical. Allow your guide to lead you to your child self. Whatever you see or encounter along the way are powerful symbols, so take note of them so you can remember them later.

You might call to your child self, they may suddenly appear in front of you, or your guide may lead you to them—or vice versa. Once you can see your child self, open your arms, welcoming the child. Allow a response, even if it is fear or cowering. Simply welcoming your child self back, out of hiding, is powerful.

This alone could complete the purpose of your ritual. But you may want to offer the child a gift or words of comfort. You might ask questions, as you would a child in real life, about their favorite toys or games. Their emotional response will give you a lot of information about your innermost self. Are they afraid? Angry? Joyous? Stubborn? Eager? Allow your child self to express these emotions, listening for messages about yourself. They may bring you toys you recall or old books you once enjoyed or sing meaningful songs. Simply observe.

Whenever you start to feel tired, perhaps with too much effort or information, thank your child self. Perhaps offer a hug. Then begin your journey back to the door. Your guide will know the way back. I recommend that this whole imagination journey last around a half hour, to start.

Phase 3: Reflect on Symbols, Feel Their Meaning, and Celebrate Insights

Like dreams, after an imaginative journey the mind can collapse what happened, and we can easily forget. So it is important to debrief, either with the friend who guided you or in a journal. Speak or write down everything you saw, felt, and encountered—in detail. Allow emotions to arise as you recall, and reflect on the sense of deep and powerful meaning that can arise. If insights arise, write them down too. Just know that imaginative images can offer a mysterious symbology of messages that may take months or years to understand.

There are many journeys to undertake in a lifetime, and the ramifications can last a lifetime. So celebrate whatever step you took, whether small or large. Life unfolds in a series of steps, and you won't take them all at once. So I invite you to visit your child self repeatedly. They may introduce you to other lost parts of yourself, or perhaps you will feel inspired to go looking for anything your trauma caused to hide. Celebrate everything you encounter along the journey of self-discovery, and you will one day realize how resilient you are.

Let Music Move You Through Anything

WE'VE ALL FELT OVERWHELMED AND BURDENED BY life. There are times when it feels like the weight upon our shoulders is unbearable. Even as we are getting through each day, determined to persevere, we can't help but experience emotional breakdowns that get the best of us. They might only last an evening, a couple of hours, or just a few moments before we might blink the feelings back. But during hardship we can quickly sink into paralyzing sadness, frantic and all-consuming panic, and a shock or numbness that leaves us staring blankly into space.

The risk is that these small emotional breakdowns can build into a real mental health crisis. So when they are happening to you regularly, take them as a sign: you need help in some form, instantly. While absolutely a therapist or loving friends and family can be there for you, ultimately we are all navigating a personal experience through life. So it's important to consider how you can help yourself.

Being able to aid yourself begins with a trigger, like one of these moments of emotional overwhelm, that is your spirit crying out for help. Then you can respond by simply asking, "What do I need?" While there are many levels of needs, you can start the process of turning around a mini-crisis moment by asking, "What music do I need to listen to right now?"

Music has the ability to guide you through anything. Similar to all people throughout time, I have experienced the profound healing effects of music in my life. Whether I need to center, focus, stimulate, or inspire myself, music can be the answer. It has led me into states of mind where I was able to gain insight into challenges, to receive important answers about my direction in life, and to find levels of strength and endurance I didn't know I had.

This power within music has led me deep into experimentation, research, and analysis. When I was introduced to drumming and watched twenty-five patients in chronic pain experience more relief than medication could provide, I had to research its effects. I participated in research that showed rhythms lower brain neurological frequencies from the anxiety-ridden, high Beta state to a Theta state of deep relaxation. Rhythms increased patients' endorphin levels during surgery so that their experience of pain during recovery was greatly eased. I have explored the effects of rhythms on all kinds of psychological states, as well as the physical body, attempting to find the precise rhythmic patterns and speeds that can restore feelings of well-being. This resulted in developing the BioAcoustical Utilization Device (BAUD) and also a whole suite of musical compositions that you can access from https://mindbodybylawlis.com and find under my name, "Dr. Frank Lawlis," on iTunes.

I recommend that you get ready for moments of mini-crises by knowing what music you will turn to when you are in need. I found that key themes within the music itself can stabilize you and offer the rhythmic support you need. Here is an overview of what I found, so you can select musical rhythms and harmonies that can heal and restore feelings of well-being.

Personal Preference: While the structures of musical compositions cause clear reactions in the brain that can be tracked with QEEG brain scans, we each react differently based on our experiences in life, personal preferences, and cultural backgrounds. So trust the songs you feel drawn to in different moments—they do have the power to enlighten and awaken your unique insights about who you are amidst your challenge.

Homeostasis: *Homeostasis* is a term that describes a balanced, steady state. When you are feeling taken over by strong emotion, knocked flat by an event, or just generally off-kilter, seek long pieces that seem to bring you home to yourself. Some people turn to calming classical piano music. Or perhaps choose a song that reminds you of your hometown or a happy moment in your childhood. Listen attentively with your eyes closed and allow the music to get your imagination going. The goal is to restore joy and energy, so you end your listening session feeling refreshed and able to face what is happening in your life.

Joy and Peace: High energy pieces, like exercise or dance music, are effective for times when your energy is low and you feel unmotivated or depressed. You don't need to pay constant attention to it, so you can listen when you are attending to other issues, such as driving around town, studying for class, or preparing a presentation.

Entropy: *Entropy* implies the randomness of energy, which is a state from which creativity arises. When you need creative solutions to big challenges, seek music that slows you down and makes you highly receptive to ideas. This suggestible state will support your ability to see how things connect, intersect, and form patterns. It can help with writer's block and discovering new practicalities to support any path you're following in life.

Awakening: When you flash back on painful, traumatizing events from your past and are overwhelmed by fears of something happening again, it helps to use headphones to stimulate the left side of the brain with melodic music for one minute. Then stimulate the right side with a harmonic music piece for another minute. Then for two minutes, stimulate both sides with melody and harmony. A "tickling" sensation that feels good is a great sign that you are recovering.

Gonging: Gonging brings you powerfully into the present moment. Striking a gong is like calling forth your inner wisdom to center your mind and body. You can find chants and guided meditations that include gongs. Allow their sound to help you focus on the present instead of regrets of the past or control of the future. This is helpful for stress about your performance in any part of your life.

Stable States: This musical sound produces a sense of space in the imagination, which inspires new perception. People listening to this type of music describe words or messages from their spiritual images, such as Buddha, Jesus, God, and others, as well as sources within themselves. Perhaps the most powerful for resiliency, this music can help you make choices to clarify your journey in life.

Sleep Training: Lack of restorative sleep can cause all sorts of dysfunctions within your brain, making it near impossible to navigate changes and challenges. The first step is to start a bedtime ritual and healthy sleep routine that includes controlling your environment, such as creating a dark place with no noises that interfere with sleep habits. But it can be difficult to sleep for eight to nine hours, especially if you suffer from nightmares. This is where music can help. For example, a music piece I called "Relaxation with Flute" can train your brain to shift from an intensively stressed Beta state to enter a relaxed Delta state. And listening to a heartbeat-like rhythm can help you feel safe and cared for enough to relax into sleep.

Humming and Toning: You can always—at any time—soothe, uplift, energize, or relax yourself by making your own sounds. Whether a favorite song arises and you hum it, or random tones come out your mouth like sighs, you cannot get this wrong. Your body will act as a tuning fork to your emotions. So give yourself permission to express your inner music naturally. It may give you the chance to transform a moment of sadness into a healing release, for example.

If this seems intuitive, you're right. It is. Music is so integrated within us that we turn to its healing power instinctively, naturally. So trust your selections, or access the ones I created, and find the rhythms and melodies you need to get through anything. I have seen so many lives change, so many people recover from hardships like addiction or mental illness, and watched those living in excruciating pain get up to dance. Incorporating music and vibrational sound with the inner work of psychology has amazed me again and again. So make music a core tool for experiencing resilience in your life.

Find the Love in Loss

Loss. Like you, I sure wish it didn't happen. But a true sign that the world operates based on a wisdom greater than humanity's is that we all die. We all lose people we love. We outlive our pets. And we each face our own mortality. It's something we don't have the ability to control. Therefore, we will all grieve losses in the course of a lifetime. All because we love people and we love life.

Grief at the loss of a loved one can overtake us. It does hurt us deeply. And the process of healing is slow and lonely. Even if we have the support of people around us, possibly a therapist, it is an internal journey of coming to terms with a profound change.

It is also painful to be reminded that our own life will eventually end. Events, especially accidents and health crises, happen with or without warning. While we have some control over how long we will live, whether through managing our diet, exercise, the stress levels we endure, the people we live with, the religious faith we have, or even denying death or accepting its inevitability, our fate is to usually die within one hundred years.

For many years, I was a counselor to cancer patients—witnessing thousands of people meet this challenge. Some continued to deny the possibility of death and sought miracles, while others suffered in fear of their future death long before they had even received a terminal prognosis. But when patients were able to accept the inevitability of death, for us all, they experienced insights in their final days that allowed them to transition comfortably, even looking forward to shedding their weak and painful body, with a sense of purpose.

Most people have faith in an afterlife, that their spirit or consciousness will continue in some way. Still, having this faith does not always lower our anxieties, nor minimize grief, when we face death among family, friends, and ourselves. While we always live with some uncertainty of the future, death makes us face it. We don't know what lies ahead for ourselves and our loved ones, even with teachings on heaven and hell, reincarnation, forever families, or what it means for someone to just not exist anymore. This uncertainty amplifies our fears and emotions, which is how loss can challenge our resilience.

I approach these facts of life with a question: Why do we tend to think of loss of life as a problem? It's going to happen, so it's more helpful to think of death as a reason to refocus on what ultimately matters most in life: love for each other and for life itself. It is the ultimate reminder to look within, sort out priorities, and live with renewed vigor. Death actually offers you the ultimate opportunity for self-discovery.

You will meet death in your own way, passing through states like anger, negotiation, depression, denial, and resolution. Coming to terms with loss is a cycle of ongoing processes. But in my experience, the level of resilience you experience when facing this loss depends on how you have faced other challenges in the past. This is how building your resilience throughout all kinds of circumstances can matter when facing its ultimate test: loss of life.

It may feel dark, or morbid, to explore the rituals in this chapter. But this is an essential part of resiliency. Honestly, I look forward to working with people on the edge of life. It is a powerful opportunity to creatively come to terms with who you are. I know because I have lost loved ones and have also been pronounced dead and survived. Death is not something to fear or deny. Instead, facing its truth is a pathway to profound messages about how to live lovingly.

A Loving Way Through Loss

When we lose a person we love, the same love that once bonded us to them can become a source of pain. We need to grieve and feel sad, sometimes deeply, and this can happen within the purity of our love. But negative emotions can poison love to the extent that it harms our ability to keep on going in our own life. So I want to share a way to release these emotions.

In loss, we often blame others—even God—for the death of a loved one. We can also blame ourselves, thinking there must have been more preventative actions we could have taken or something different we could have done. You might grow angry or replay the last moments you spent with your loved one over and over again in your head, seeking some kind of explanation or trying to identify what went wrong so you know who to blame. This kind of blame feels gritty, and you may even come up with substantial evidence against someone else, God, or yourself, but it is like dry sand running through your fingers. Truly there is no one to blame for what happened.

It's true that someone may have caused a death, inadvertently or with malice. But revenge is no resolution. Vengeful thoughts whittle away at the beauty and appreciation of virtually everything you hold dear. They will harm you much more than they'll harm anyone else.

You don't need to get stuck in this chapter of your life. A forgiveness ritual will help you turn the page. Forgiveness does not relieve another person or higher power of responsibility; instead it resolves the vengefulness and guilt. Don't poison your love for someone who has passed. Instead, carry this love forward as a part of the purpose and destiny of your life. Here's a ritual you can do.

1. Find a secluded space where you won't be interrupted. Light a candle or incense, perhaps rinse your hands and face, or connect with a natural surrounding. This will mark the opening of this ritual. Then set the intention to relate with a wisdom greater than your ordinary, thinking mind.
2. Gently connect with your feelings of blame. Then write a letter to yourself, another person, or the higher power you feel let this tragedy happen. Tell whomever, or whatever, you blame exactly what you are feeling and thinking. Get it all out. The goal is to express so much that you don't need to keep rehashing it in your mind because you have written it all down in this letter. You can add to the letter over the course of several days.
3. When you feel complete, you may need some time to let things settle. You will know when you are ready to release blame because there will be a flicker of hope in life. You might catch a glimpse of time and life marching on, steadily, toward a future without your loved one in it.

4. Take some time to retreat and call on the elements, similarly to how you did in chapter 1, for help with releasing blame. Take the letter and offer it to the elements: burning it with fire, letting it drift away into water, tearing it into pieces and throwing it into the wind, or burying it in the earth.
5. As you do, feel the sensations of letting go that precede forgiveness. You'll notice a long exhale, a sense that a weight is lifted, or your muscles might relax.
6. Then say, out loud, "I forgive you." See how that feels.

Forgiveness has the power to purify feelings of love. This is important because love will help us navigate this change with resilience. As we come to terms with a change we don't want, thousands of questions arise. Be suspicious of all the ones that start with "Why . . ." Trying to answer the question, "Why did they have to die?" is a sign that you are still hurting. A helpful way to ensure you stay on a healing track, and don't descend into blame, is to honor your loved one by celebrating them. Still, memorials, donations, flowers, and gathering to celebrate a life are most powerful when you focus on the feeling of love. We bond deeply when grieving, and while everyone will feel the loss differently, doing it together is a beautiful part of being human.

Doing this will also keep you open to learning about yourself and what life is showing you as you heal. Perhaps you will come to appreciate someone in ways you overlooked, or took for granted, during their lifetime. Maybe it's now time to learn to offer yourself what they gave you. It's true that you can continue to relate with, and learn from, people after they are gone. By staying tuned into love, you can continue to feel the impact and meaning of someone's life. I feel this is the most potent way of honoring them.

With love at the center of your attention, you can also stay in a healthy frame of mind as you mourn. Grieving a loss takes time, usually around a year. During then, you will experience powerful emotions that need to be felt. These emotions are not abnormal. While you don't want to let them overcome you completely, you also don't want to stuff or ignore them. If you do, a day will come when those suppressed feelings will surface—even decades later.

Grief is resolved through a slow process of emotional integration, especially as anniversaries of important events in life with our loved one come and go. You will always miss them. And sadness at this loss can come up, and then pass, for the rest of your life. But don't let it interfere with your own life celebrations. Joy and sadness are feelings that can coexist, just as you are physically capable of laughing and crying at the same time. Always remember that your loved one wanted you to be joyful in life, so finding new sources of meaning and purpose after their passing would fulfill the deep wish they harbored for you.

Love in Your Life, Love at Your Death

Have you faced death and survived? If so, you most certainly came back from the brink with messages that changed you, or your life, somehow. Overwhelmingly, people who nearly die report that the experience had powerfully beneficial impacts on them. The messages in their experiences come in many forms, whether seeing holy light, being surrounded by departed loved ones, or feeling profound peace. I have heard them all describe levels of love that could wash away all fears. They return and know just how their lives need to change.

Even though I can make a few generalizations about this, it is such a personal experience that the only way I can fully share what I know about facing death is to offer my own story. There was a time when I felt pretty miserable in my life. I had reached a dead end with my career as a university professor when I became president of a small graduate school in California. I was also in a marriage that had supported my professional rise but had lost any sense of being a source of comfort and love.

One morning, as I prepared for a lecture in health psychology, I felt strange and clumsy. I walked out of the classroom to get air, and passed out. I had a terminal heart attack. Yes, you read that right. I died to the world, to the point that a friend called my wife to announce my demise and advised her to wear a widow outfit.

During the time I was considered dead, I was in another zone somewhere between life and death. It was an amazing experience that is impossible to put into words. All I can verbalize is that I felt pure love and compassion surrounding me. There were no demands made on me, only to learn to receive this "sweetness of love." I just absorbed it.

Time disappeared, so I have no clue how long this lasted. Then I woke to a couple of medics nursing me. They told me I had been dead to their devices . . . until I awoke. I felt amazingly well, so I dismissed them, only to be told that I absolutely had to go to the hospital. After arguing heatedly with the medics, two police officers appeared so I jumped up, ran downstairs, and buckled myself into the driver's seat of the ambulance. The medics had to coax me into the treatment area. At the hospital, I was labeled a "rebellious patient" until the chairman of the cardiac program was able to convince me of the seriousness of my condition. The love I felt while dead infused me to the point that I still felt no fear. After a short stay in the hospital, I was released with a rehabilitation lifestyle to restore my heart (which was not damaged).

Here's what's most important about my story. My heart knew I was on the wrong path in life, and it sent me a clear message. So I declared that I was through with my job and California. I told my wife that I would be leaving the state and going to New Mexico, and she could come with me if she wanted. I felt like a new person with a new chapter for my life. More than two decades have passed since then, and my heart has remained strong.

While life since then has had many twists and turns, that memory of overpowering love has never left me. Having witnessed the other side of life, I know what awaits me . . . and it is beautiful. This knowledge is a potent source of resiliency for me. Now I face death as an elderly man, which gives me more vulnerabilities and limits. But I am still not retired, and I am eager for the next chapters in life. Struggling in life has strengthened my resilience because it always reminds me of my personal mission of service. While I have work to do in my life, knowing that love transcends death inspires me to honor my time to pass when it comes.

Awareness of our own death and accepting its inevitability not only has mental health benefits, it also encourages us spiritually. It inspires us to live in a truer way, aligned with our purpose and what is most important to us. So I want to share a ritual you can do to relate with death. It's oddly one of the most cheerful and motivating experiences you can have. It doesn't matter what your beliefs about the afterlife are; you will benefit from this awareness now.

I have used this ritual for people who are in chronic pain or are inhibited by physical ailment to the point that they can no longer function according to the way they use to or according to society's expectations for them. I have found that the level of abandonment people in this situation feel, whether they were fired from jobs or their family gave up on them, is like experiencing a death. They need to die to their old sense of self to be reminded that they are still valuable to others and themselves. They need a new source of self-respect, or there could be no resiliency for their lives.

In the same way, all of us need to take a step back from who we think we are. You can do it purposefully, before an accident or illness strikes to mandate your attention. Events don't need to be so extreme. Instead, you can live with awareness of death and do this ritual regularly to reap the benefits. Here's what I recommend.

1. Play a recording of rhythmic drumming, turn off the lights, spread a blanket on the floor, and lie down on it, perhaps with a pillow under your knees. Get comfortable. Take a few moments to relax your muscles, from your feet to your head.
2. When you are ready, imagine being at your own funeral or memorial service. Your casket or urn is in the front of the room. People you know are there, some are speaking and some are silently reflecting. Visually observe the scene for a moment.
3. Imagine that a loved one, whether family member or friend, gets up to speak about you. What do they say? Listen as different people share their sense of your life. Consider these questions:

- Listen as they bring up any themes that characterize your life. What are the themes? Are people's perceptions about you accurate?
- Listen to them describe your actions. Consider their views of your behavior and choices in life. Are they aligned with your inner motivation for doing these things?
- Do the things people say about their experiences with you align with your deepest desires for how you want to live?
- Have you been living in ways that fulfill your expectations for yourself?
- Now that you have a more distanced perspective on yourself, by imagining other people's experiences of you, would you change your life?

4. In your imagination, thank the people who spoke. Whatever they said, feel love for them—for being part of your life and coming to your funeral to honor you. Close this ritual with a moment of appreciation.

When I, and my patients, do this ritual, we gain a lot of feedback about the purpose of our lives. As we listen to our loved ones speak, most of us are shocked at the level of disconnection between what our intentions for life are and how others see us—or don't see us—living these intentions in what we do and say.

Stay with this shock and get out your journal. Write down all the ways you feel disconnected from living out what's important. Perhaps list them, or dig into memories, or set down your insights. Eventually, when you decide to live more in alignment with what's most important for your life, and your purpose, this writing will be like a menu of the changes you can make.

A key to resiliency is realizing that before you can make positive changes in your life, you need to know how *you* need to change inwardly. Learning and growing as a human being is a beautiful intention to have in your life. It can help make so much happen, in ways that will survive longer than you do. Consider the legacy you want to outlive you, because you will live on through what you accomplish, as well as in the hearts and minds of the people you contact. So take a long view, to your death and past it, and help build a world that supports what's most important to you.

Gather Resourcefulness from Inspirational Stories

Say you're riding along in life, as if you're on a bicycle. You slip on a mud patch that you didn't see and down you go. There is the pain of impact and scratches from the pavement. You sit stunned. You might call for help. You might start to cry. But eventually you realize that the only way to arrive home—where you most what to be—is to get up, get back on your bike, and keep on riding. You'll get home eventually, maybe late and bruised, but you'll not only have reached your goal—you'll have a story to tell. One that humanity has told a million times and never tires of sharing. The story of resiliency.

Every one of us is filled to the brim with stories to share. And we are eager to hear each other tell them. We watch them in movies or television, read them, and play them out in computer games because stories ultimately remind us of who we are and what we're capable of doing. They're so powerfully rooted in basic human nature: We are all born storytellers, within any culture, at any time in history. We have an innate hunger for them, so we can learn from them. That's why we surround our children with stories—not only do they love them, it's how we share our values as individuals and a society. Stories have an influence that goes further than just reflecting how we live; they also form our awareness of who we are.

When we communicate with each other, we're often telling stories that consist of a person facing challenges and some kind of problem. This human tale is about facing the issue, gathering resources to engage it, and then struggling to overcome the challenge. Whether it's a story of survival where someone's life is on the line, about an important relationship that develops cracks in the bond holding two people together, sharing what happens when a group unites to further a political or social cause they care about, or even a person facing their own harmful behavior, our stories make heroes of everyone alive.

Have you ever paused to consider how you are the hero of your own stories? You have the human story coded within you: to be a hero, you must stand up to your challenges resiliently. Even if you are a day-to-day hero, responding to your emails and texts, helping your children navigate their world, relating to the complexity and frantic pace of life while pursuing your goals, it all boils down to being responsive to each day's challenges. That is resiliency.

So what do you do when life events take away something you love, you feel like you just can't face a problem, can't cope, balls you've been juggling are falling all around you, and you're so exhausted and depleted that all you want is to crawl into a cave? It can feel like you're living out a hundred mini-stories in one day. Sometimes it's just too hard to keep going, or keep up, and be a hero for them all.

This is why we need stories. You need to know that we're in this project called life together. You can learn from what happened to others to understand what is happening to you.

Your life experience can also comfort and teach others. It's a virtuous spiral of benefit, this dance of being human. So here are ways you can fuel resiliency with stories.

Seek Role Models

With stories, you don't need to personally know role models and mentors for them to make a difference in your life. You can turn to movies, biographies, and documentaries to learn about all types of people who achieved amazing things. Ask yourself:

- Who made a difference in the course of history, in ways I admire?
- Who lived out values that align with mine?
- Who demonstrated character traits that I want to cultivate in my own life?

Personally, I look to George Washington for the wisdom of knowing himself amidst the temptations of power, which led to a humble greatness. Abraham Lincoln was not well liked for his ideas, but his resilience stirred hearts and minds toward the highest ideals of brotherly care and support. When I could use life advice, I often read about people who lived in service to causes greater than themselves.

What have people you admire accomplished? Do you know the story behind it? If not, get curious and find out. Their example might offer solutions to your own struggles.

Seek Inspiration and Motivation

Through the course of history, humans have accomplished amazing feats. Some of them took hundreds of years and many lifetimes, and other inventions changed the world seemingly overnight. If you are challenged by a goal, and it feels too far away to reach, or the sacrifices to get there are too demanding, turn to stories for inspiration and motivation. If others did it, so can you.

Seek Self-Understanding

Sometimes, fantastical tales of faraway lands and stories of an ordinary being rising to meet an extreme need—like the threat of a population's decimation—can remind you what our spirits are capable of doing. These stories are not only grand adventures, they are also character studies. The hero struggles internally along the way, battling doubts and other inner obstacles just as vividly as foes with swords or laser guns. As a result, you can witness a hero's way of resolving inner setbacks to accomplish great things. You might find your own way forward that is meaningful to your life and your resiliency.

Seek Knowledge of Your Roots

Family stories can tell you about who you are, how you experience life, and the ways you tend to respond to it. Consider the legacy, within history's grand scope, that culminated in your birth. Ask your elders to tell stories about the past. And seek a deeper understanding of things you experienced in childhood, from the perspectives of your parents and caregivers. All this will help you perceive the strengths that got your family through hardship and that are most likely within you too. What can you draw on? Is there a character trait that has been handed down to you? Or perhaps a member of your family inspires you, which is a powerful personal tie to turn toward in times of struggle.

Stay True to Your Story

Resiliency involves returning to your self as your primary guide. If you're busy living out someone else's story, and not your own, challenges will not feel worth the effort. For example, if you deep down feel a sense of mission to be nurturing and supportive to others, you aren't likely to be willing to work as hard as a capitalistic boss, hell-bent on increasing profits, would want you to. If your personal goal in life is to serve people's spiritual needs, it doesn't make sense to put a ton of effort into maintaining luxurious appearances. Many of our favorite stories are about a person achieving high levels of success in the world, only to realize how empty they feel. They might return to their small hometown to serve a loving purpose, perhaps with close family and friends who get through it all together: the highlights, the pain, the successes, and the mistakes.

So in your retreat time, consider the story you are living. And ask: *Is this who I truly am? Can I be the hero of this life . . . or am I working against my efforts by living out something that's not true, that doesn't reflect my core desires for my life?* Then consider what different story you want to live. It will have challenges, but they will be worth all the hard work it takes to overcome them.

Tell Your Own Hero Story

You have been through so much already; it's guaranteed. And you have more to go through. So the essential skill to develop, right now, is how to discover your greater self again and again—rediscovering it whenever you lose sight of who you are. You are alive; therefore, you're the hero of your story. So I recommend that you write down your heroic tales. If you want to share these with others, great. If not, you will be able to turn to them in the future if you forget what you are actually capable of doing.

You don't need to have saved the world to be a hero. Your heroism can take so many forms and give you a sense of purpose. Heroic acts can mark large turning points in life, like moving to a new town, getting out of an abusive marriage, switching careers to something more fulfilling, and surviving a difficult childbirth. But like my opening story about falling off a bicycle, it is heroic to get back up, dust ourselves off, and keep going. Everyday efforts count. You might even like to write them down daily, in the evenings. Get curious about how each day's resiliency has made you a hero today.

Observe Your Plot Twists

Once you start writing your hero tales, you'll be able to see the plot twists that have happened in your life. Life is a journey of discovery, in any moment. Sometimes you'll hear a word, take on a new task that becomes a quest, or an accidental occurrence—a coincidence—strikes at the right time. These can all cause the course of your life to change . . . and become a plot twist in your story.

Benjamin was a young man I was counseling, who was a car thief. He refused to stop stealing fancy cars, especially Corvettes, and he was facing serious jail time. To him, driving downtown in a red Corvette made him feel proud and important. He was determined to chase that feeling, but he didn't have any money and with his criminal history didn't have much hope of ever being able to purchase a flashy car. So he kept stealing them. One day, I asked Benjamin, "How else can you gain the admiration and respect you need?" No answer came.

But life had an answer for him. It came as a plot twist

when Benjamin saw a child drowning. He jumped into the pool and saved the child's life. Suddenly, he was a hero in so many eyes—especially his own. He started trying to succeed in life, joined a running club, and won a race. These successes helped him realize that there were many paths he could take in life. He could steal cars or choose helpful ways to feel proud and important. His life's plot twists changed him for the better, and he joyfully decided to get a teaching degree instead.

All stories are filled with events, and some determine the fates of the characters. What has happened in your life that determined its course? By looking at these plot twists, you can gain insight into what's most important to you. This can determine your future.

As a professional counselor, I have heard many profound stories of courage and resiliency from patients that continue to inspire me. I have heard tales of marriage conflicts that only the deepest love could get through. People have faced job changes that caused tremendous anxiety, that contradicted personal values, and that croded confidence in ways that caused my heart to bleed—until patients started prioritizing themselves over financial gains. Most of all, I love self-discovery stories of patients overcoming the anguish at having stepped outside themselves, losing self-respect for the sake of life goals that were not theirs.

I get excited when I hear stories of people finding peace and joy within themselves. But this usually comes after a big challenge that rattled them to the core. Our basic human story illustrates the power of resiliency: it builds the strength that will help greater things happen in the future. Make this come true for you.

Continuously Spiral Toward Growth

DISEASES OF ALL KINDS RESULT FROM IMBALANCES in the body. Most often "health" is defined as the absence of disease, but the truth is that only very rarely do we ever exist without some form of imbalance. So what is true health? I believe that it is a state in which we have resources to protect ourselves from the effects of imbalance, such as lifestyle choices, helpful treatments like massage or acupuncture, and medications. Similarly, when it comes to our mental and spiritual health, resiliency arises from having the resources to protect us from the effects of imbalance.

We actually need to be challenged and gain strength at every stage of our lives, in a growth spiral. Yes, you will always be moving forward through time, but this growth process does not happen linearly. You can be going along, doing well in life, and then suddenly say something happens like a loose dog comes running toward you in a park. Suddenly in your mind you are three years old, terrified because a dog attacked you then. Those old feelings are still with you, waiting to be healed. So as an adult, can you grow into a new way of being? Can you see that today's dog is wagging his tail and just wants to lick you and be petted? That shift is a moment of healing, of growth. It happens in a spiral as you are invited to revisit old feelings again and again, learning something fresh each time.

More significantly, we all live in a spiral of forgetting who we are and what's important to us. You need frequent calls back to your core self so you can remember and access your Inner Compass. This is why challenges are not burdens, but gifts: they give back your self through reminders to turn inward and look. What you discover will change and grow too, so that when you step forward in life again, it will be at a whole new level. This is the nature of a growth spiral. When you view your life this way, with resiliency, you will be able to uncover, accept, and navigate your true destiny.

Growth spirals show up in many forms, and I'll offer two examples of them so you can learn to see when they're happening. The first is based on human life cycles. And the second is how vices become virtues.

The Learning Stages of Life

As you grew up, you passed through five learning stages. While these do correspond with phases of human development, you are constantly revisiting these lessons so you can grow. There are infinite ways of unpacking and deepening life's messages, just as there are infinite choices you can make as a result. It can help to recognize what a specific challenge is guiding you to reconsider and learn right now. Here are the five basic life lessons you will spiral through repeatedly.

Survival: The first challenge of life starts before we are born, when we have to survive. It continues whenever the basic needs in life are threatened: access to food, water, shelter, and healthcare. These things are sadly not a given in life, and so sometimes we find ourselves in a position where we depend on others. Asking for help, and receiving it, can be a survival tool.

Self-Identification: The next stage of learning is self-identification, when we learn to define ourselves against the backdrop of other people, objects, and creatures. We learn our name, how to write it, and especially to be accountable for what we do. We absorb what it means to be part of our particular family. And eventually most of us need to come to terms with being different from our family too, as an individual with a personal calling and style.

Love and Affection: The bonds we have with our parents and caregivers determine a lot about how we will continue to engage people we love. If the styles of those bonds caused pain, such as abuse being confused with love, things can get distorted, and eventually we need to learn new ways of relating. There are many different expressions of love and affection that we can develop, and expanding these feelings is a powerful lifelong journey.

Communication: How we express ourselves can vary based on each relationship we form. But underlying it is the degree to which we can trust people to accept who we are. If we face a lot of judgment in life, including outright discrimination, we will be careful with how much of ourselves we share. Still, we all desire to be seen and accepted, so being able to authentically communicate calls for ongoing growth.

Spirituality: It's often said that the world works in mysterious ways. This causes us to seek answers and turn to spiritual paths that help us relate with things beyond our control. Often, if we try to live without spirituality, we get shaken awake by a disaster that we can only get through if we turn to a power greater than us. And when we become too focused on mundane or material matters, we also receive reminders to turn toward our spirituality once again.

Whenever we think things have become totally clear and we start to live among clouds and rainbows, expecting constant joy, something happens to bring us back to earth—and to this growth spiral. It starts over again so we can learn anew. Each time, the spiral is different and hopefully deeper-reaching, unfolding according to mysterious cosmic timing.

Changing Vices into Virtues

Cycles of change are natural. And so is choosing the wrong road to travel. Sometimes, vices result when you lose yourself and your Inner Compass. Loss of overall energy and turbulent emotions can cause us to act out, whether against others or ourselves.

When we turn against ourselves, whether out of disappointment, rage, self-blame, regret, loss, or hopelessness, we can cease caring about survival. This is when someone can't stop thinking about their own death. There is so much darkness and fear because we can feel completely lost in life. The psychic pain makes us isolate, so we lose all sense of promise for living. Then it seems the only path that offers release from the pain is death. Even when we reach this dire state, it can be a time for powerful enlightenment. Trust in change. Trust in words of love and compassion, for they will find their way to you. Your brain can listen and form new neurological pathways. Each small hope builds to the next, and pain will release its hold on you. Resilience is this built into our neurology. So never, ever give up hope because your brain and body can grow past anything.

You can think of this process as a growth spiral. We enter an extreme state of mind . . . then something happens, within or outside us, to pull us out of it—often drawing us toward its opposite. While we may feel pulled back into darkness, again the light shines and we shift. Then the next time we feel the pull of something, such as the extreme sadness and hopelessness of depression, we also feel the pull of joy as we see our children playing or even birds flying by. We know there is happiness and joy in life, and slowly we spiral our way free from sustained depressive feelings.

A similar thing happens when we turn against our self-interest through habits of thinking and acting that are limiting, distorting, or distracting. We can become so obsessed with anything that there is no room in our lives for positive learning and growth. Unhealthy obsessions are common in our complex society, and they ultimately strengthen our weaknesses. Humanity has as many weaknesses as strengths, so to illustrate my point about how growth spirals work, I'll turn to two wisdom traditions, Christianity and Buddhism.

In the classic Christian list, the seven deadly sins are psychological traits that the wisdom of early thinkers countered with seven heavenly virtues.

Deadly Sins	Heavenly Virtues
Lust	Appreciation
Gluttony	Simplicity
Greed	Charity
Sloth	Diligence
Wrath	Patience
Envy	Gratitude
Pride	Humility

Just like the example of a growth spiral I gave for depression, you can work your way out of any of these sins, as you are also naturally drawn toward its virtuous opposite. It starts in small ways . . . and grows. By noticing the urge to be wrathful, you can take a deep breath and wait. When you write the tip on a receipt, you can notice greed—and still add a couple more dollars. If you're feeling pride about an accomplishment, look around and thank someone who supported the effort too. It isn't like you will go to sleep envious and wake up grateful the next day. Instead you can transform your life through a growth spiral, going back and forth between states of mind as more virtuous pathways in your brain form. Then true changes happen and continue to increase for the rest of your life.

Another way of thinking about this comes from ancient Buddhist teachings that describe non-virtuous traits as causes of suffering. Releasing yourself from suffering is a learning process that works to transcend mistaken ideas about who our self is. So a key part of the Buddhist path is practicing the six paramitas, or "transcendental actions." These are generosity, discipline, patience, diligence, meditative concentration, and wisdom. By intentionally performing these actions, your mind can be pulled closer to an enlightened state, free from suffering. Because non-virtuous thoughts, feelings, and actions continue to arise, each time you become aware of them in daily life, you can choose a paramita response instead. Doing this repeatedly, over time, strengthens and expands the mind of enlightenment. This offers another way you can use the growth spiral to transform hardship into a path of self-discovery.

Here's some advice to live by: The best prediction of the future is that it will change. There is always a tomorrow, and you can bet it will be different. You can always wait and see, always smell a fresh smell, see a beautiful sunset, sing a new song, and watch life work its ever-changing magic. Even words you have heard before can sound different on another day. This is how you can—and already do—create new realities for yourself. It's an adventure of a lifetime to learn new things, especially about yourself.

Each one of us has to live our own life. Your will is not all-powerful, but your Inner Compass is because when you are following it, you will know how to get through obstacles and challenges. Life is precious, and along the way you will encounter your own weaknesses. Mistakes will be made. But if you are mindful of each step, the power of the growth spiral will turn those mistakes into wisdom.

Try seeing the life lesson in all challenges. While the cycles of the spiral differ in urgency and opportunity, you will begin to meet challenges eagerly because you know that growth awaits.

Conclusion

The Enduring Secret of Self-Discovery

I LIKE TO GET AT THE HONEST TRUTH ABOUT LIFE. It has challenges around every corner that can be really hard to endure. We each face unique obstacles in our unique way, and it's nobody's fault. We live in a complicated world, so getting through life is a creative dance that's up to you. Your life is going to develop in unpredictable ways that defy your plans. You are going to encounter your weaknesses and make mistakes. This makes your time on earth a grand adventure.

From birth you have carried a mission for your life. While the path is winding, missteps are common, and challenges extreme, you will feel satisfied when you know you're on track with this mission. As long as you are learning and growing, following your Inner Compass, you're on track to fulfill your soul's purpose. We are naturally resilient beings. Within you, you have everything you need.

But you probably forget this along the way, often. We all do. We easily become disconnected from ourselves, which leads to low energy and motivation, loss of joy, and even a misery that can be subtle and also excruciating. This especially happens if you have not truly struggled much in life because you have never been stripped bare—down to your soul—and been forced to ask important questions. Material wealth can actually be a curse when life is so pleasurable and easy that you don't truly know who you are. I have met people who don't know hardship in their lives. And I have concluded that we simply must suffer if we are to experience the kind of happiness that is authentic and enduring.

Your challenges ultimately can become ongoing sources of great joy, positive energy, and true happiness that lasts a lifetime—no matter what happens. The secret to reaching this level of resilience in your life is clear. Make the journey into an epic adventure through self-discovery. Then you will always emerge stronger because challenges have become opportunities to know more about who you are—which fuels everything you do. The result of finding yourself in this way is true happiness. So please, do me and the world a favor: find your bliss.

Further Reading

Achterberg, J. (1991) "Transpersonal Medicine: A Proposed System of Healing," *ReVision* 14: 127

Achterberg, J. and Lawlis, F. (1979) "A Canonical Relationship between Blood Chemistries and Psychological Variables in Cancer Patients," *Multivariate Experimental Research*, (4)

Achterberg, J. and Lawlis, F. (1979) *Imagery and Cancer*, Champaign, IL: IPAT

Achterberg, J. and Lawlis, F. (1980) *Imagery and Disease*, Champaign, IL: IPAT

Achterberg, J. (1985) *Imagery and Healing*, Boston: Shambhala

Achterberg, J. Lawlis, F. and McGraw, P. (1985) "Treating Rheumatoid Arthritis with Relaxation and Biofeedback," *Therapeutic Practice in Behavioral Medicine*, San Francisco: Jossey-Bass

Achterberg, J. (1991) "Ritual: The Foundation for Transpersonal Medicine," *ReVision*, Vol. 14, No. 3, 158-64

Achterberg, J. (1994) "Healing Images and Symbols in Nonordinary States of Consciousness," *ReVision* 16, no. 4, 148-56

Benson, H. (1975) *The Relaxation Response*, New York: Morrow

Campbell, J. (1976) *Creative Mythology*, New York: Penguin Group

Doore, G. (1998) *Shaman's Path*, Boston: Shambhala

Dossey, L. (1989) *Recovering the Soul*, New York: Bantam

Frankl, V. (1960) *The Doctor and the Soul*, New York: Knopf

Harner, M. (1980) *The Way of the Shaman*, San Francisco: Harper and Row

Ingerman, S. (1991) *Soul Retrieval*, New York: Harper Collins

Lawlis, F. (1994) *The Cure*, San Jose: Resource

Lawlis, F. (1996) *Transpersonal Medicine*, Boston: Shambhala

Lawlis, F. (2016) *An Imagery Pilgrimage through Symbolic Challenges toward Health*, Amazon

Lawlis, F. (2006) *The IQ Answer*, New York: Viking

Lawlis, F. and Martinez, L. (2016) *Animal and Nature Rituals*, Amazon

Leshan, L. (1974) *The Medium, The Mystic, and the Physicist*, New York: Viking

Levine, S. (1989) *Healing into Life and Death*, New York: Anchor

Lindsey, C. and Lawlis, F., (1988) "Effectiveness of Imagery as a Childbirth Preparatory Technique," *Journal of Mental Imagery*, 12 (1)

Penrose, R. (1994) *Shadows of the Mind*, New York: Oxford University

Maslow, A. (1968) *Toward a Psychology of Being*, Princeton, NJ: Van Nostrand

Maxfield, M. (1994) "The Journey of the Drum," *ReVision* 16, No. 4, 157-63

Rider, M. and Achterberg, J., (1989) "The Effect of Music-Mediated Imagery on Neutrophils and Lymphocytes" *Biofeedback and Self-Regulation*, 14, no. 3

Rider, M. (1992) "Mental Shifts and Resonance: Necessities of Healing?," *ReVision* 14, No. 3, 149-57

Rodgers, C. (1960) *On Becoming a Person*, Boston: Houghton Mifflin

Rossi, E. (1986) *The Psychology of Mind-Body Healing*, New York: W.W. Norton

Lightning Source UK Ltd.
Milton Keynes UK
UKHW020645280322
400716UK00007B/201